Presented
to

_____

From

_____

date_____

MY FRIENDS THE SAINTS

**Illustrated Prayer-Talks
with Favorite Saints**

By

Rev. Lawrence G. Lovasik, S.V.D.
Divine Word Missionary

CATHOLIC BOOK PUBLISHING CO.
NEW JERSEY

CONTENTS

Nihil Obstat: Francis J. McAree, S.T.D., Censor Librorum
Imprimatur: ✠ Patrick J. Sheridan, D.D., Vicar General, Archdiocese of New York
The Nihil Obstat and Imprimatur are official declarations that a book or pamphlet is free of doctrinal or moral error. No implication is contained
therein that those who have granted the Nihil Obstat and Imprimatur agree with the contents, opinions, or statements expressed.

(T-270)

MARY, MOTHER OF GOD

Queen of All Saints

Died 1st century A.D.   January 1—August 22

DEAR Mary, loving Mother of God,
Queen of all Saints and help of Christians,
come to the aid of your children on earth.

You are the most blessed of all creatures
and the most beloved by Jesus.

You are my Mother also,
and I am devoted to you.

I am most grateful
that Jesus gave you to me
to be my Mother, my Helper, and my Protector.

SAINT ELIZABETH ANN SETON

Forerunner of the Modern Christian Woman

1774-1821   Feast: January 4

- Born in America—Mother, Widow, Religious
- Left a Widow with five children
- Became a Catholic with deep trust in God

- Founder of first American teaching order of nuns
- Initiator of the American parochial school system
- Deeply concerned with the welfare of children

FORERUNNER of the modern Christian woman,
dear Saint Elizabeth Ann,
you served God in many walks of life.

Born in New York into a Christian family,
you had a happy marriage and raised five children.

When your husband, William Seton, became ill,
you went with him to Italy where he died.

In your sorrow, you turned to Catholic friends,
and they welcomed you into their home.

Returning home, you became a Catholic
and opened the first parish school in America.

You founded the Sisters of Charity,
inspired many women to follow you,
and became the first American-born Saint.

Grant that I may have some of your love for God
and your deep concern for others.

Help me to be like you and to follow Jesus
whenever and wherever He may call me.

SAINT JOHN BOSCO
Apostle of Youth

1815-1888   Feast: January 31

- Born in Italy into devout Christian family
- Became priest — father and teacher of the young
- Wrote books and booklets to spread the Faith
- In time of need called upon the Virgin Mary
- By prayer and Sacraments brought the young to God
- Loved by children because he cared

YOUR parents, dear Saint John,
lived on a farm and were very poor.

You became a priest dedicated to helping young boys,
especially orphans and runaways.

You established schools to teach boys trades,
and soon your boys were going out into the world
as successful craftsmen and model Christians.

And you combined new educational techniques
with love for God
to lead young people closer to Christ.

To continue your work you founded
the Salesian Orders of Priests, Brothers, and Nuns
to assist boys and girls.

Throughout the whole Catholic world,
you are known as the Apostle of Youth.

In our world today,
there are still runaway boys and girls.

Help me to have a special love for them
and to assist them in any way I can.

SAINT MARGARET OF CORTONA

Model of Penitents

1247-1297   Feast: February 22

- A native of Italy and a Single Parent-Penitent
- Did penance in public for past sins
- Turned life around by prayer and good works
- Extraordinary love for the Crucified Savior
- Heroically served sick as Franciscan Tertiary
- Died after 29 years of performing penance

MANY trials filled your life,
dear Saint Margaret.

Your mother died when you were seven years old,
and your stepmother had little care for you.

Rejected at home, you ran away with a young man
and gave birth to a son without being married.

When you returned to Cortona,
your father refused to accept you and your son,
but the Franciscan Friars gave you shelter.

You joined the Franciscan Third Order
and drew close to Jesus by prayer and penance.

And your son joined the Franciscans
a few years later.

You served the sick poor and by word and example
brought many people back to God.

Help me to be sorry and repent
whenever I do anything that offends God
and always trust in His great love and mercy.

SAINT PATRICK

Missionary for Christ

390-461   Feast: March 17

- At sixteen sold as slave to Irish chief
- Turned to God and learned to pray
- Escaped and became a priest
- Ordained Bishop and sent to Ireland
- Suffered opposition from the pagan druids
- Planted seed of Faith throughout the land

OUR heavenly Patron, Saint Patrick,
you brought many people to Christ.

Many of their descendants in turn
spread the Good News to other people.

You established monasteries for men and women
and made Ireland famous
as a center of learning,
and as a place where people lived their Faith.

Soon Irish monks carried the Faith
to England, France, and other parts of the world.

In my prayer,
I make use of your words:

As I arise today,
may the strength of God pilot me,
the power of God uphold me,
the wisdom of God guide me.

May the hand of God protect me,
the way of God lie before me.

11

SAINT JOSEPH

Patron of the Universal Church

Died in 1st century A.D.   **Feast: March 19**

- From noble ancestry of Abraham and David
- Carpenter at Nazareth— known as a just man
- Heart full of love and self-sacrifice
- In Bethlehem with Mary at birth of Jesus
- In Egypt with Jesus and Mary as refugees
- Died in arms of Jesus and Mary

O GREAT Saint Joseph,
you were the husband of the Virgin Mary
and foster father of Jesus.

During your life on earth,
you were always obedient
to the guidance of the Holy Spirit.

Watch over me every day
just as you watched over Jesus
when He was growing up.

Obtain for me the grace to know
what God wants me to be in life,
because my happiness on earth depends on it.

Help me to carry out God's will faithfully
and to choose the vocation
that will lead me to heaven.

Protect the Church throughout the world
and assist all who labor for souls
amid the trials and tribulations of this life.

SAINT CATHERINE OF SIENA

Counselor to Popes

1347-1380   Feast: April 29

- Born in Italy—called to be peacemaker in Church and civil affairs
- Meditated often on Christ's Passion
- Bore His wounds on her own body

- Her wise counsel was sought by many—even the Pope
- Convinced Pope to return from Avignon to Rome
- One of only two women Doctors of the Church

A WOMAN of great faith and wisdom, Saint Catherine,
at twelve you dedicated your virginity to God.

Your parents wanted you to marry,
but when you persevered in your resolve
to give yourself entirely to God, they agreed.

You spent much time in prayer and penance
and became a Dominican Tertiary.

You were often seen feeding the poor,
nursing the sick, and visiting those in prison.

You are among the greatest spiritual writers
for you were united with God through frequent prayer.

But you were also involved in human affairs,
seeking to bring peace to Europe and to the Church.

Your last days were full of suffering,
which you offered up for all Christians.

Help me to walk in your footsteps
by a life of prayer and service for the love of God.

SAINT RITA

1381-1457   Feast: May 22

- Born in Italy—desired religious life
- Entered an arranged marriage and became good wife and mother
- When widowed, joined Augustinian Sisters
- Possessed deep love for the Crucified Savior
- On her forehead had wound like thorn from crucifix
- Powerful intercessor for us with God

MODEL wife and widow, Saint Rita,
you were a devoted follower of Jesus
although you suffered greatly in your life.

Your husband often mistreated you,
but he died at an early age,
and so did your two sons.

Now you were alone in the world.
But prayer, penance, and good works
filled your days.

Then you entered the Augustinian convent
and began life as a Religious,
a life of perfect obedience and great charity.

You were afflicted with a long illness,
and you accepted this crown of sufferings.

With deep trust in God alone,
you overcame all your troubles.

Obtain for me the grace to trust God in all things
and keep me and my loved ones safe in God's care.

17

SAINT JOAN OF ARC

Teenage Soldier of God

1412-1431   Feast: May 30

- Born in France—often spent time in prayer
- At seventeen was called to defend country and Faith
- Led soldiers carrying a banner with the words "Jesus, Mary"
- Filled with courage, her army defeated the enemy
- Was captured and then condemned to death
- Was burned to death with the Name of Jesus on her lips

WILLING Soldier of God, Saint Joan,
at the young age of seventeen you heard God's will
in the voices of His Saints
telling you to defend your country against enemies.

You had a great love for Jesus
Whom you often received in Holy Communion.

You always proclaimed: "Let God be served first,"
and you won many victories for the cause of God
and for the people of France.

You then fell into the hands of enemies
and were cruelly put to death
at the young age of nineteen.

Help me to serve God first
and carry out my earthly tasks
with that idea ever in my mind.

Let me love my country and its people
and pray that it may always be a source
of wisdom and strength, order and integrity in the world.

SAINT ANTHONY OF PADUA

Patron of the Poor

1195-1231   Feast: June 13

- Born in Portugal of rich parents
- Became poor for Christ as Franciscan
- As preacher had gift to touch hearts
- Brought many sinners back to God
- Infant Jesus appeared to him
- Performed miracles— known as Wonderworker

KNOWN as the miracle worker, Saint Anthony,
you are the patron of the poor
and the helper of all who seek lost articles.

You devoted yourself to the work of preaching,
for you were an exceptional orator
filled with zeal for souls.

So numerous were those who flocked to hear you,
that no church could hold them.
And you had to preach in the streets and fields.

You also taught us the importance of prayer,
which puts us in touch with God
and brings us His help.

Keep me close to God each day
through my daily prayers.

Help me to be good to my family
and all my friends.

Assist all who seek what they have lost,
especially those hoping to regain God's grace.

SAINT PETER THE APOSTLE

The First Pope

Died in 64 A.D.   Feast: June 29

- A fisherman of Galilee named Simon
- Called by Jesus, became His follower for life
- Name changed to Peter the "Rock"

- Gave first public Apostolic sermon at Pentecost
- First Bishop of Church and first Pope
- Under his guidance Church spread rapidly

WHILE fishing, dear Saint Peter,
you were called by Jesus
and you left everything to follow Him.

You were chosen to do our Lord's work
of bringing people to God.

One day, Jesus asked the Apostles,
"Who do you think I am?"
And you replied without hesitation,
"You are the Messiah, the Son of God."

Jesus changed your name to Peter, which means "Rock."
You were the Rock on which He built His Church.

Jesus gave you the keys to the Kingdom of Heaven,
making you the head of the Church and the first Pope.

You gave the rest of your life to our Lord
and showed your love to the end,
for you died preaching the Name of Jesus.

Help me to give my life for Jesus
and do all that I can to spread the Good News.

BLESSED KATERI TEKAKWITHA

Lily of the Mohawks

1656-1680   Feast: July 14

- Born in New York of the Mohawk tribe
- Embraced the Faith as a teenager
- Accepted cost—hostility of the tribe
- Went to Christian colony of Indians in Canada
- Each morning even in bitter cold went to Mass
- One of the first Native American Christians

LILY of the Mohawks, Blessed Kateri,
you suffered much from illness
and you suffered even more
when you became a follower of Christ.

You were dedicated to prayer and penance
as well as care for the poor,
the sick, and the aged.

You were devoted to the Eucharist
and to the Cross of Jesus
up to the very end of your short life.

Obtain for me a true devotion to the Blessed Sacrament
and help me to prepare well
for receiving Jesus in the Eucharist.

Let me always thank Him
for giving His life on the Cross
to gain heaven for me and for all people.

Teach me to treat all people as children of God
regardless of their race or religion.

SAINT MAXIMILIAN KOLBE

Apostle of the Printed Word

1894-1941   Feast: August 14

- Born in Poland—and became Franciscan
- Had extraordinary love for Mary Immaculate
- Spread devotion to Mary by writings

- Founded communities dedicated to Mary
- Imprisoned during Nazi invasion
- Died taking the place of a fellow prisoner

GLORIOUS Advocate of Mary, dear Saint Maximilian, you established a worldwide movement to honor her.

You labored under her patronage to spread the Faith in Japan and India by means of the printed word until poor health forced you to return to Poland.

During the Nazi invasion, you preached God's Word and suffered severely in a concentration camp.

When ten inmates were condemned to death, you imitated your Master, the Son of Mary, and laid down your life for one of them.

You gave us a striking example of love for Christ and for our fellow human beings that cannot be surpassed.

And since you died not many years ago, you show us that sanctity is still possible even in our own day.

Obtain for me a strong devotion to Mary and unselfish love for God and neighbor.

SAINT AUGUSTINE OF HIPPO

Outstanding Father of the Church

354-430   Feast: August 28

- Born in North Africa—to a half-Christian family
- As a youth led a life of pleasure-seeking
- Converted by prayers of his Mother Saint Monica
- As a Bishop of Hippo, preached the Faith
- Religious genius and thinker still read today
- His "Confessions" and "City of God" are classics

GIANT of the Catholic Faith, dear Saint Augustine,
you first learned it from your Mother, Saint Monica,
who was married to a non-Christian.

You were drawn to fleshly recreation,
yet you felt an inner longing that was unsatisfied.

As a result of your saintly mother's prayers,
your father became a Catholic on his deathbed,
and you were baptized by Saint Ambrose in Milan.

Returning to Africa, you became a priest
and then were elected bishop by the people.

You enriched the Church with writings and sermons,
defended the Faith against false teachings,
and wrote about your conversion and the spiritual life.

Now your longings were fulfilled and you could say,
"You have made our hearts for Yourself, O Lord,
and they are restless until they rest in You."

Help me and all Christians to thirst after God
Who alone can satisfy our restless human hearts.

SAINT VINCENT DE PAUL

Apostle of Charity

1580-1660   Feast: September 27

- Born in France—and ordained a priest
- Sensitive to needs of others
- Established new Religious Orders to serve the poor
- Remained ever humble despite worldly acclaim
- Taught that the Church must help the neediest
- His Society continues his work in our day

THE mere mention of your name, dear Saint Vincent, suggests charity—helping the poor and needy.

As a priest, you were dedicated to serving the poor, and you built many homes for abandoned children as well as for the sick and the aged.

To further this work, you laid the foundations for the Vincentians and the Sisters of Charity.

You organized lay people in parishes to help the needy, something the Saint Vincent de Paul Society continues to do throughout the world today.

You zealously conducted retreats for the clergy at a time when there was great laxity.
And you established many seminaries that formed priests who were educated and caring.

Though extremely active in works of charity, through prayer you remained united with God.

Help me to imitate your kindness to the poor and to do all I can to help those in need.

SAINT THERESA OF THE CHILD JESUS

The Saint of the Little Way

1873-1897   **Feast: October 1**

- Born in France to loving Christian parents
- Had ardent desire to save souls
- Offered prayers and sufferings for souls
- Followed "Little Way" of trust in God
- Did little things to please God
- Only twenty-four when called to heaven

KNOWN as the Little Flower, dear Saint Theresa,
from childhood you desired to be a spouse of Christ.

You entered the Carmel of Lisieux at age fifteen
and began a life of spiritual childhood—the Little Way.

This consisted in love of God as a Father,
expressed in childlike simplicity and trust,
and a deep understanding of the Cross.

You suffered much, especially from tuberculosis,
but you offered it for the conversion of sinners
and the help of priests, particularly missionaries.

Shortly before your death you said
you would spend your heaven in doing good on earth.

Your mission would be to teach others
the way of love, trust, and self-surrender to God.

And you had a fervent, intense love
for the Blessed Virgin Mary.

Teach me your Little Way of childlike trust in God
and help me to offer little things to Him each day.

SAINT FRANCIS OF ASSISI
Saint of the World

1181-1226   Feast: October 4

- Born in Assisi—as youth sought good times
- Attracted by Knighthood and military valor
- In a dream told to serve the Master
- Abandoned worldly ways and lived life of the poor
- Told by Jesus, "Build up My house"
- His Franciscans brought message of joy to all

BECOMING poor for the sake of Jesus,
dear Saint Francis,
you showed love for all God's creatures.

For two years you lived as a hermit
near San Damiano's church.

You begged for your food
and for the materials to repair the old church.
Then you set about to build up Christianity itself.

Establishing the Franciscans to spread the Good News,
you brought many people back to God.

You had great love for Jesus Crucified
and received the imprints of His Wounds in your body.

You also started the custom of the Christmas Crib
to bring His people closer to our Lord.

Help me to love Jesus with all my heart,
remind me to show concern for all God's creatures,
and let me do what I can to keep the environment clean,
making the world safe for everybody.

SAINT TERESA OF AVILA

Teacher of the Spiritual Life

1515-1582   **Feast: October 15**

- Born in Spain—joined the Carmelite Order
- Called to return the Order to its original simplicity
- Was wise yet practical; prayerful yet an energetic reformer
- Knew value of suffering for God and desired it
- Her teachings on spiritual life show love for God
- Recognized as excellent spiritual writer and noted Doctor of the Church

RELIGIOUS common sense, dear Saint Teresa, was one of your finest gifts from God.

As a member of the Carmelite Order in Spain, you were called by God to reform the Order, which had lost much of its original vigor and fervor.

Starting your own convent, you taught the nuns the ways of fervent prayer and self-sacrifice.

Then you traveled throughout Spain, founding new convents and reforming others and suffering greatly from some who opposed you.

You led a life of profound union with God, combining intense prayer with vigorous action.

And you wrote works teaching the way of perfection, which is the way of the Cross.

These writings earned for you the glorious title of Doctor of the Church.

Help me always to be a good Christian and not become lax in loving and serving God.

SAINT FRANCES CABRINI

Apostle to Immigrants

1850-1917   Feast: November 13

- Born in Italy—as girl worked on family farm
- From childhood wanted to be a missionary in China
- On Pope's advice came to America to serve Italian immigrants

- Brought them comfort and strengthened their faith
- Tried only to please God and to work for His glory
- To her nothing seemed beyond human strength aided by grace

YOUR life, dear Saint Frances Cabrini,
truly shows that God works in mysterious ways.

At eighteen, poor health kept you from becoming a nun,
so you were content to work on the family farm
and later to teach in a girls' school.

Later, at the bishop's request,
you began the Missionary Sisters of the Sacred Heart
to care for poor children.

Pope Leo XIII advised you to go to America
and render service to the Italian immigrants.

Beginning in New York, you worked tirelessly
to help immigrants overcome the obstacles
of language, customs, and prejudices.

You went on to build orphanages
as well as schools, and hospitals in America and Europe
and became the first American citizen to be canonized.

Help me to assist all immigrants
as my brothers and sisters in Christ.

SPECIAL FRIENDS OF GOD

THERE are many, many Saints in heaven—
men and women, boys and girls.

Jesus told us how we could recognize His followers.
He said we are His disciples if we love one another.

So love is the sign of a true Christian.
And the Saints are those who loved most
and persevered to the end.

Their love was reflected in their actions.
They always helped those in need.

It is good for us to read
about our Friends the Saints.
This will inspire us to be like them.

And we should ask their help in all our needs,
for they are special Friends of God.

MAGNIFICENT EDITIONS THAT BELONG IN
EVERY CATHOLIC HOME

FIRST MASS BOOK—Ideal Children's Mass Book with all the official Mass prayers. Colored illustrations of the Mass and the Life of Christ. Confession and Communion Prayers. **Ask for No. 808**

PICTURE BOOK OF SAINTS—By Rev. L. Lovasik, S.V.D. Illustrated Lives of the Saints in full color for Young and Old. It clearly depicts the lives of over 100 popular Saints in word and picture. **Ask for No. 235**

MY FIRST PRAYERBOOK—By Rev. Lawrence G. Lovasik, S.V.D. Beautiful new prayerbook that provides prayers for the main occasions in a child's life. Features simple language, easy-to-read type, and full-color illustrations. **Ask for No. 205**

THE MASS FOR CHILDREN—By Rev. Jude Winkler, OFM Conv. New beautifully illustrated Mass Book that explains the Mass to children and contains the Mass responses they should know. It is sure to help children know and love the Mass. **Ask for No. 215**

LIVES OF THE SAINTS—New Revised Edition. Short life of a Saint and prayer for every day of the year. Over 50 illustrations. Ideal for daily meditation and private study. **Ask for No. 870**

CATHOLIC PICTURE BIBLE—By Rev. L. Lovasik, S.V.D. Thrilling, inspiring and educational for all ages. Over 110 Bible stories retold in simple words, and illustrated in full color. **Ask for No. 435**

St. Joseph FIRST CHILDREN'S BIBLE—By Father Lovasik, S.V.D. Over 50 of the best-loved stories of the Bible retold for children. Each story is written in clear and simple language and illustrated by an attractive and superbly inspiring illustration. A perfect book for introducing very young children to the Bible. **Ask for No. 135**

The STORY OF JESUS—By Father Lovasik, S.V.D. A large-format book with magnificent full colored pictures for young readers to enjoy and learn about the life of Jesus. Each story is told in simple and direct words. **Ask for No. 535**

WHEREVER CATHOLIC BOOKS ARE SOLD